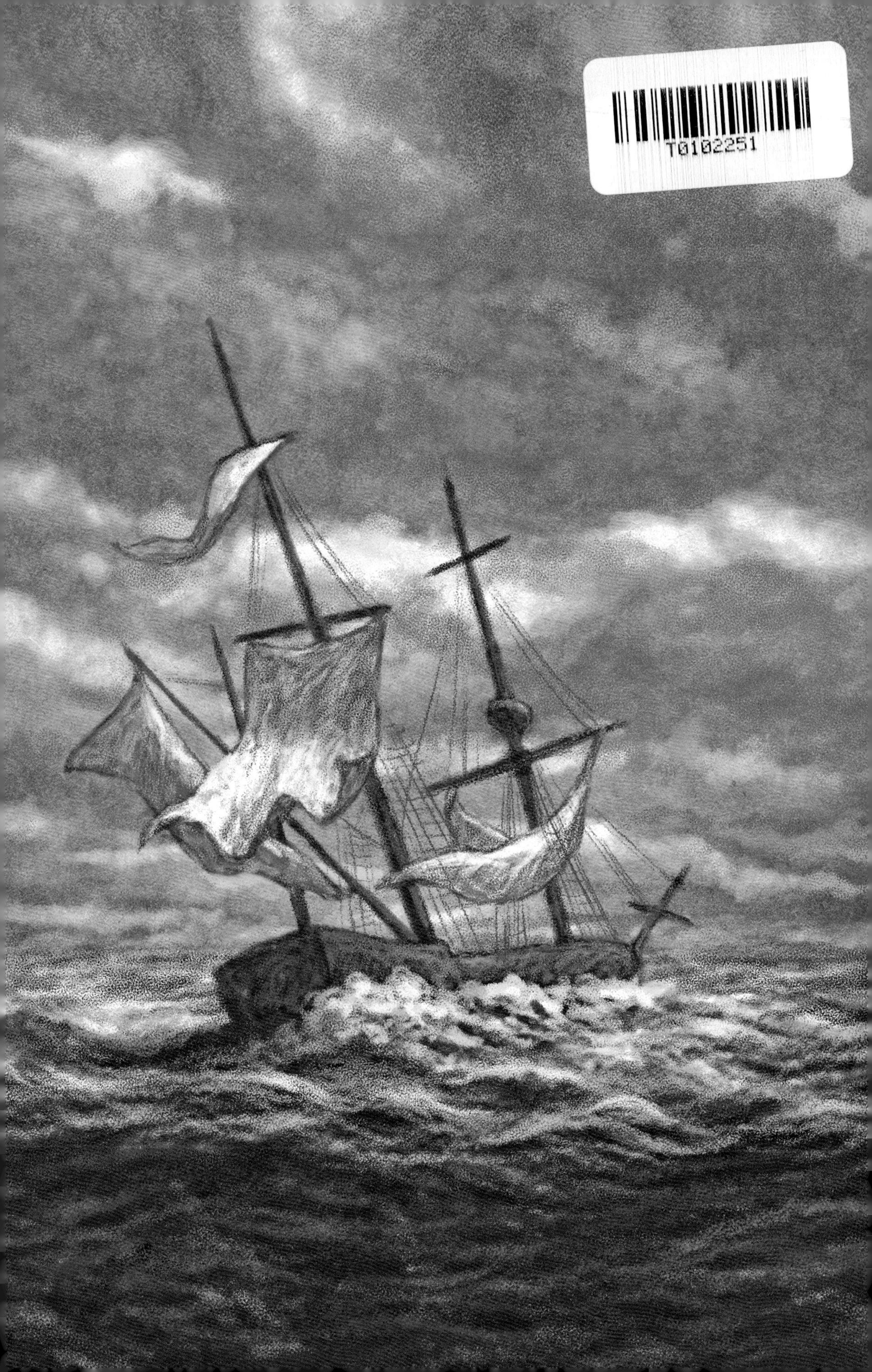

For my "Fuzzies"—Donna Miller & Vicki Marshall. Loved.
—Barbara Joosse

For Anne and Mark Schoenenberger
—Renée Graef

Published by the Wisconsin Historical Society Press
Publishers since 1855

The Wisconsin Historical Society helps people connect to the past by collecting, preserving, and sharing stories. Founded in 1846, the Society is one of the nation's finest historical institutions.
Join the Wisconsin Historical Society: wisconsinhistory.org/membership

Publication of this book was made possible in part by a grant from the Alice E. Smith fellowship fund.

Printed in the United States of America
27 26 25 24 23   1 2 3 4 5

Library of Congress Cataloging-in-Publication Data

Names: Joosse, Barbara M., author. | Graef, Renée, illustrator.
Title: Death's door : true tales of tragedy, mystery, and bravery from the Great Lakes' most dangerous waters / by Barbara Joosse ; illustrated by Renée Graef.
Description: First edition. | Madison : Wisconsin Historical Society Press, 2023. | Audience: Ages 8–11 | Audience: Grades 4–6
Identifiers: LCCN 2023007859 (print) | LCCN 2023007860 (e-book) | ISBN 9781976600159 (paperback) | ISBN 9781976600166 (e-book)
Subjects: LCSH: Porte des Morts Passage (Wis.)—Comic books, strips, Etc—Juvenile literature. | Frontier and pioneer life—Wisconsin—Comic books, strips, etc—Juvenile literature. | Shipwrecks—Wisconsin—Porte des Morts Passage—Juvenile literature.
Classification: LCC F587.P83 J667 2023 (print) | LCC F587.P83 (e-book) | DDC 977.5/6--dc23/eng/20230419
LC record available at https://lccn.loc.gov/2023007859
LC ebook record available at https://lccn.loc.gov/2023007860

♾ The paper used in this publication meets the minimum requirements of the American National Standard for Information Sciences—Permanence of Paper for Printed Library Materials, ANSI Z39.48-1992.

Death's Door

True Tales of Tragedy,
Mystery, and Bravery
from the
Great Lakes'
Most Dangerous Waters

by Barbara Joosse • Illustrated by Renée Graef

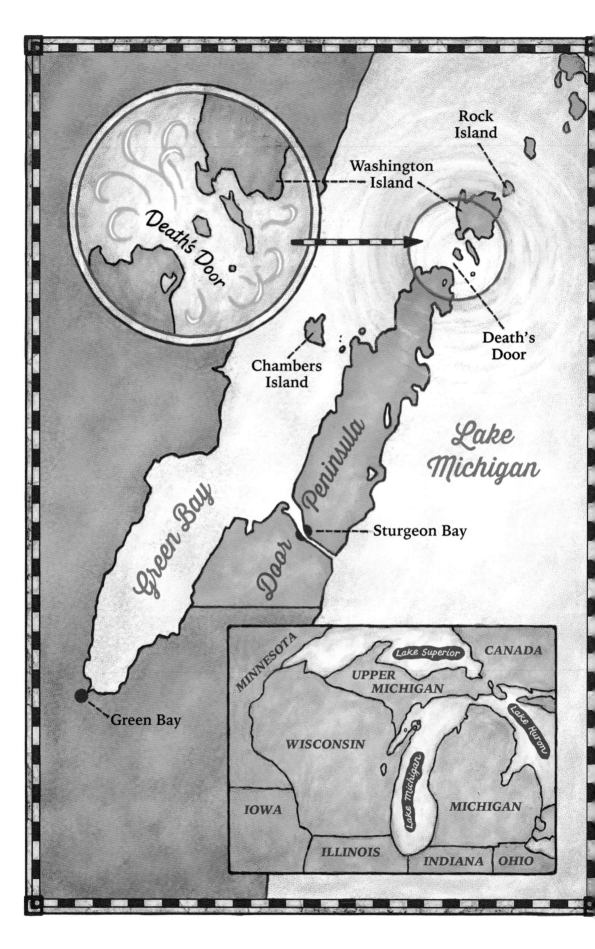

Death's Door

Rock Island

Washington Island

Death's Door

Chambers Island

Door Peninsula

Lake Michigan

Green Bay

Sturgeon Bay

Green Bay

MINNESOTA

Lake Superior

CANADA

UPPER MICHIGAN

WISCONSIN

Lake Huron

IOWA

Lake Michigan

MICHIGAN

ILLINOIS

INDIANA

OHIO

I am wind.
I am water.
I am rocks so sharp
they can tear a boat apart.

I can't help what I am.
I am Death's Door.

Long have I wondered why?
Why *do* people cross my water,
knowing of ragged rocks and wicked wind?
Listen. Look. Think.
The answers lie in their stories.

A Story of a MONSTER BATTLE

Who
Potawatomi Families

When
Probably between 1690 and 1763

Where
Death's Door

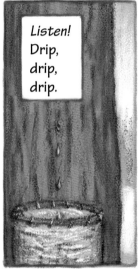

Listen! Drip, drip, drip.

The People wait till sap trickles into buckets,

till corn is planted,

till tiny sprouts pop above the earth.

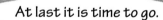

At last it is time to go.

Everyone chatters with excitement as they pile furs into canoes and pile in families, too. They're eager for the bustle of the trading post, to hear what's new and trade their furs for beads, tools, and food.

The families paddle for many days.

Sometimes they toss offerings of tobacco into the hungry mouth of the great water monster, Mishepeshu, who lurks beneath my surface, ready to pounce. Ready for war with the Thunderers.

Surely tobacco will satisfy the monster.

One blue-sky day the People stop to rest on a rocky shelf,

with a tall bluff to their backs to shelter them from the wind.

I watch as they eat bear fat and corn,

then stretch their legs in the sun, drowsy with food.

And I worry.

With sudden fury, the western sky turns black!

Listen!

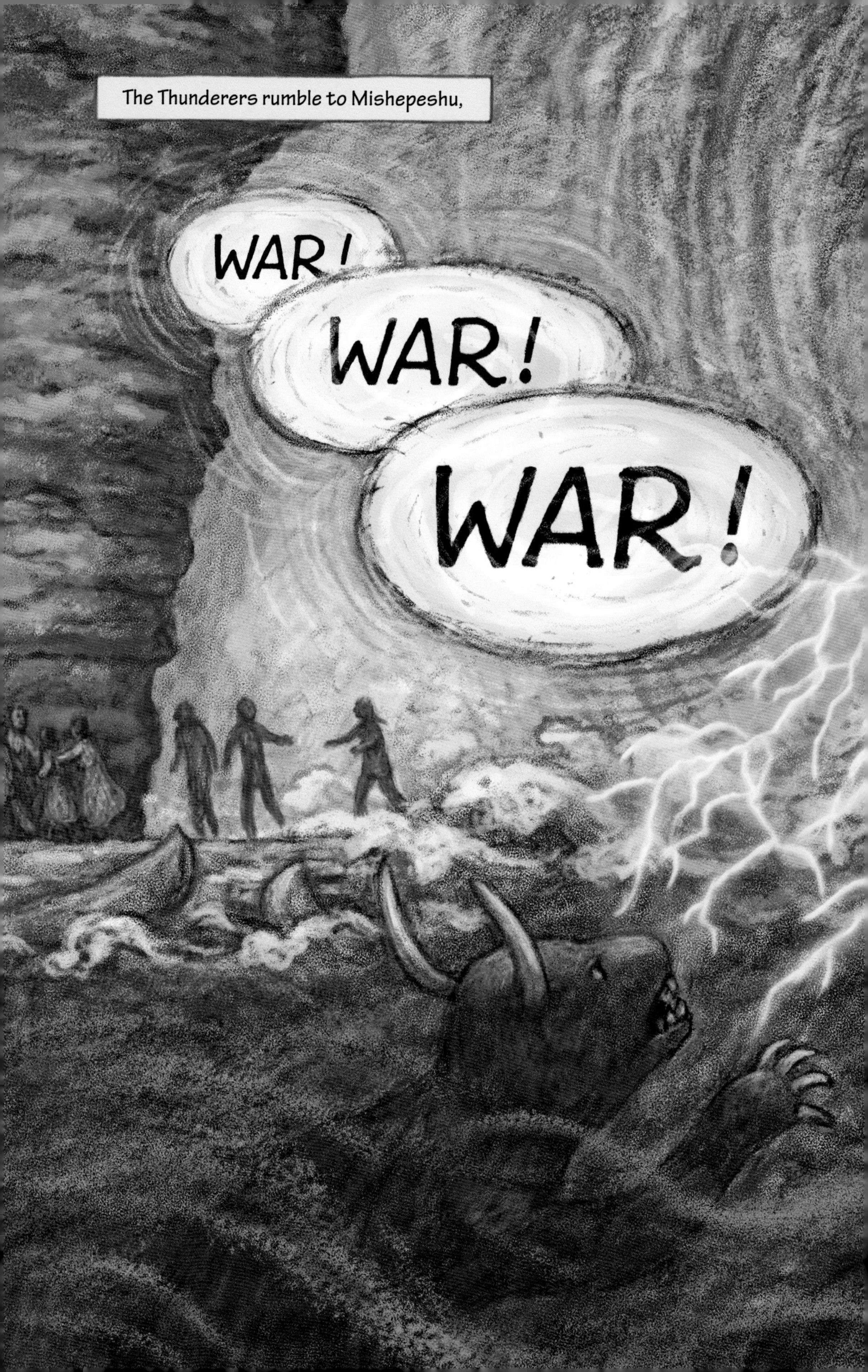
The Thunderers rumble to Mishepeshu,
WAR!
WAR!
WAR!

and shoot bolts of lightning from their eyes. My water churns as Mishepeshu and the Thunderers thrash in a terrible battle. The canoes are dashed to pieces. The People are trapped between towering waves and a bluff so steep they can't climb to safety. Many die. Innocents. The casualties of war. Forever, I will remember.

And so it was I became known as . . . Death's Door.

A Story of GREED

Who
René-Robert Cavelier,
Sieur de La Salle

When
1679

Where
Somewhere off
Rock Island

René-Robert
Cavelier, Sieur de
La Salle is a
man with a
big name . . .

and bigger
ambition.

La Salle is building a
ship—*Le Griffon*.

He borrowed money to
pay for his expeditions.

Like hungry wolves, men beat on his door to be paid.

But La Salle can't afford to pay them back!

Blind with desperation, he hatches a plan. He'll send a crew to Rock Island.

There, they'll trap and trade for piles of fur—

mountains of fur!

—then load it all onto *Le Griffon* and return to the East where La Salle can sell it.

Think.
Desperate people are often foolish. La Salle treats his workers badly, and they grumble.

He hires an untrustworthy navigator.

To save money, he hires a crew that's much too small, then works them much too hard.

At Rock Island, the trappers load valuable beaver pelts onto *Le Griffon* and grumble about low pay and extra work.

La Salle stays behind, planning to meet up with the boat later.

Groaning with the weight of La Salle's treasure, *Le Griffon* sets sail.

But La Salle never sees his crew,
his ship, or his furs again.
Le Griffon disappears

poof!

into thin air.
La Salle loses his fortune.

Where are the bones
of *Le Griffon* now?

I am Death's Door and I will not tell.
I have secrets to keep in the cold and the deep.

A Story of DUTY

Who
Mail carrier
Henry Miner
When
Winter 1856
Where
Washington Island to
Green Bay and back

Listen!
As Henry pushes his
empty sled across my
surface, the ice rings
beneath his footsteps.

Piiiing!

It's
stone
bone
cold.

Cold enough to numb a man to sleep. But Henry is the mail carrier,
and he'll walk two hundred miles to deliver the mail, news, and
supplies . . . because that's his job.

Henry thinks of his neighbors. It's been a long, cold winter on
Washington Island. For three months, the islanders haven't
received fresh supplies, news, or mail.
Nothing.
Nothing at all.

Henry nibbles molasses and fat pork as he crosses my snow-swept surface, finally reaching land.

He stops at Ole Larson's the first night,

then Bob Stephenson's the next.

After three days,

he arrives

in Green Bay.

A blizzard blows in, but Henry doesn't let it stop him!

In the swirling snow, he loads his sled with mail and supplies. Now he is ready for the trip back.

Feel it! It's thirty degrees below zero!

Henry tightens his fox-skin cap. The north wind cuts like a razor as he plows through the snow, pushing the loaded sled back toward the island. His knees ache and tremble.

After ten hours,

Henry stumbles

. . . and falls.

Completely and utterly exhausted, he can't get up. But Henry's all alone. There's no one to help.

Henry digs deeply within himself and finds a little spark of life. He lies across the sled and claws his way through the snow with his mittened hands.

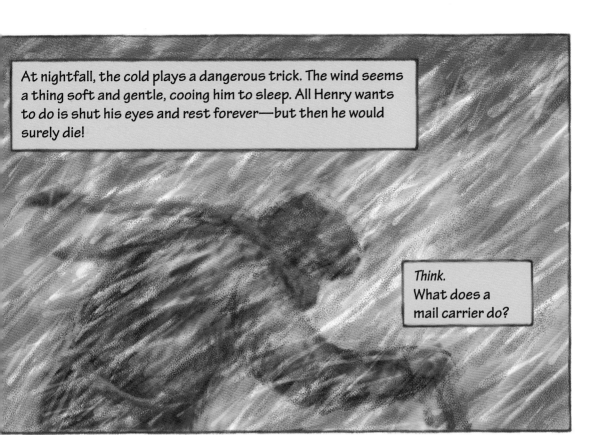

At nightfall, the cold plays a dangerous trick. The wind seems a thing soft and gentle, cooing him to sleep. All Henry wants to do is shut his eyes and rest forever—but then he would surely die!

Think.
What does a
mail carrier do?

Henry heaves up and staggers once more through the snow.

Then—can it be?

The light of a cabin ahead?

Yes! Yes, it is! Shelter! And a warm fire! Perhaps a supper of venison and carrots. Henry can almost taste it.

But when Henry arrives at the cabin, he hears shouting and crashing. The men are fighting inside—and they refuse to let Henry in!

People can be cruel, but they can also be kind. Two different men shoulder Henry's sled and guide him to another cabin and good people who welcome Henry inside.

There, Henry feasts on bear meat, then lies down before a flickering fire and sleeps.

And afterward? What does a mail carrier do?

Henry sets out once more for Washington Island.

After three more days, he arrives with a sled full of mail, newspapers, fabric, jackknives, and fishhooks.

Mail carrier Henry Miner has done his duty.

After eight days of wind and cold, Henry's story will long be told.

A Story of LOVE

Who
Sarah and David Clow

When
1862

Where
Chambers Island

Look!

A woman perches on a tree balanced on a tall trestle, whip-saw in her hands. Sarah and David Clow are building a ship. Together. Just the two.

They want their ship to carry wheat and lumber across my water and over the Great Lakes, to bring their large family honor and income.

Their snug little cabin, the first on Chambers Island,

is filled with a tumble of children and the smell of venison stew.

There's a lot of work to do at home— tending a garden,

laundry, mending,

churning butter, cooking.

But there's also time for fun! It's a fine thing to hear the children's laughter, busy with work and play. Sarah and David's laughter, too, for they find merriment in all that they do.

It takes a long time to build a ship when there are only two of you.

Trees must be cut,

stripped,

and hauled into place.

Sails sewn.

Hardest of all is raising the towering masts—tall enough to scrape the clouds!—and wedging them into place.

Captain David Clow warms with love at the sight of his wife working at his side.

Think!
What can a man give to the woman he loves? What can he give to the mother of his children, who built a home in the wilderness . . . *and is now building a ship?*

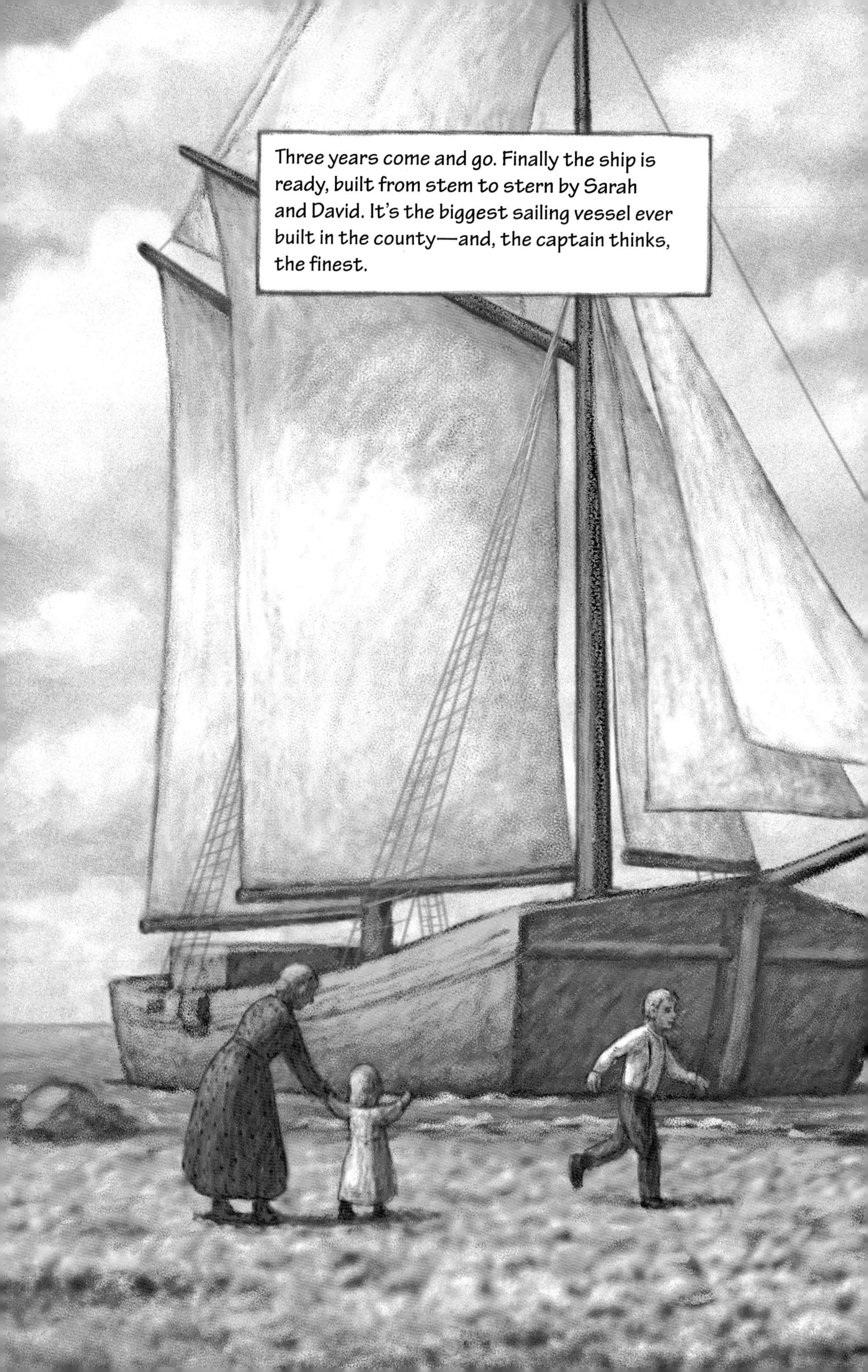
Three years come and go. Finally the ship is ready, built from stem to stern by Sarah and David. It's the biggest sailing vessel ever built in the county—and, the captain thinks, the finest.

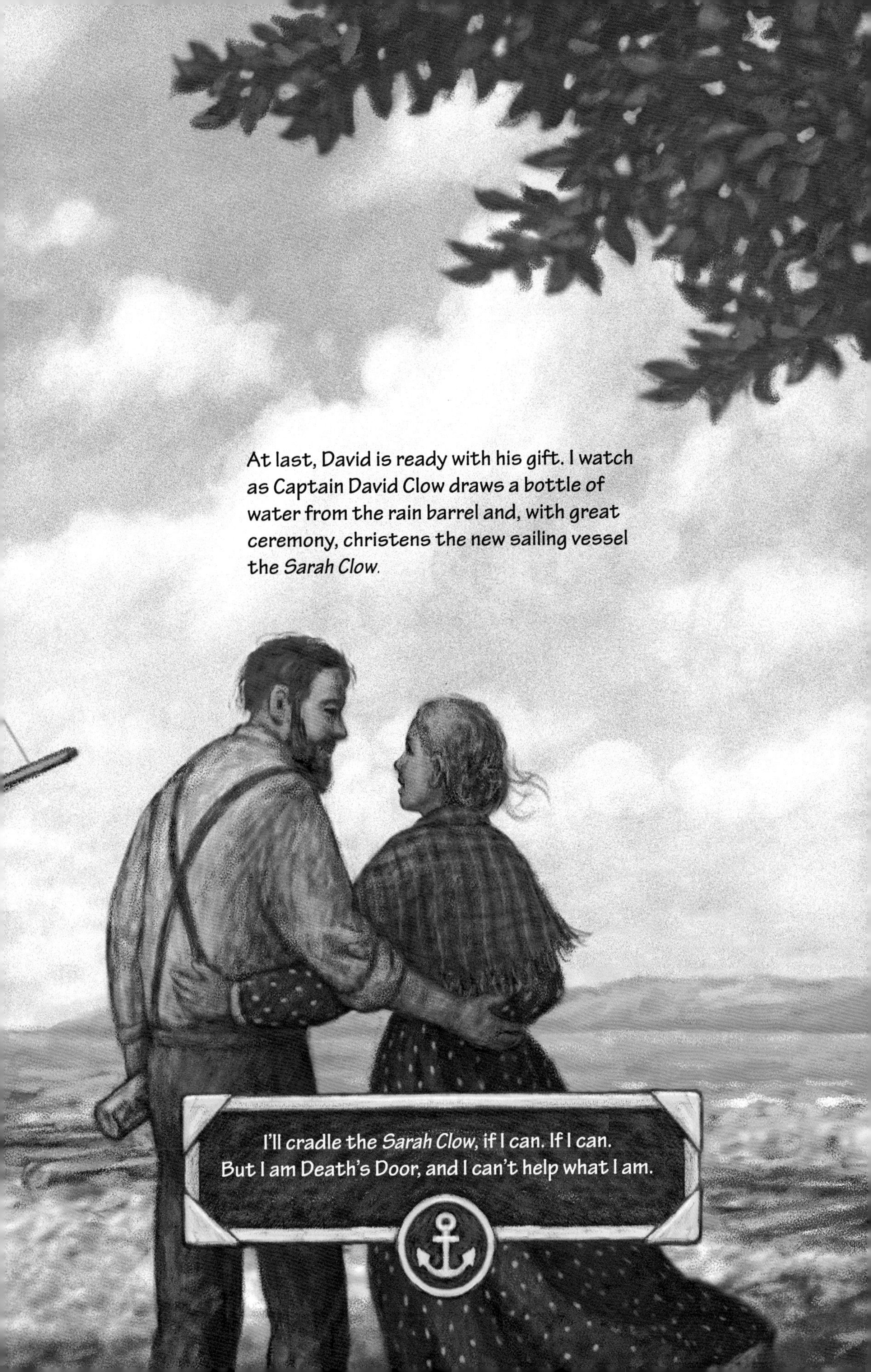

At last, David is ready with his gift. I watch as Captain David Clow draws a bottle of water from the rain barrel and, with great ceremony, christens the new sailing vessel the *Sarah Clow*.

I'll cradle the *Sarah Clow*, if I can. If I can.
But I am Death's Door, and I can't help what I am.

A Story of CABIN FEVER

Who
Washington Island men's basketball team

When
March 1935

Where
Death's Door

Feel it!

The creepy-crawlies, like mosquitos buzzing under your skin.

Like you can't stand one more minute on the island,

one more minute of cold,

one more minute

staring at the walls of your room.

The islanders call it cabin fever—a kind of winter madness,

a hunger for adventure just as real as the hunger for food.

It makes people burst out of their homes, their safe places.

For adventure.

For fun. For something new.

Nearly everyone on Washington Island has cabin fever.

And the cure?

A car trip across my crystal bridge—the icy passage to the Door Peninsula.

To a basketball tournament.

To whooping and hollering and celebrating the end of old man winter.

But late-winter ice is thin and dangerous. So I worry.

Players, coaches, and fans pile into cars.

They know what thinning ice can do and the safest passage to take this time of year. They know it's best to travel together in a caravan, so that's what they do.

The game is a klunker. The Ellison Bay Aces hammer the Washington Islanders, 57–18.

The islanders spend the night in Sturgeon Bay. They agree to meet in the morning and drive back over the ice together.

But the next morning, only six men gather at my shore— the coach and five players, not the rest of the caravan.

Maybe the others are sleeping in. Maybe they got their signals crossed. But the men don't want to wait.

They crowd into the coach's car and drive into the fog, alone.

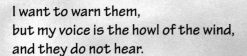

I want to warn them,
but my voice is the howl of the wind,
and they do not hear.

They're in a hurry and
take a short cut.

But they never make it home. A search party spies their tire tracks and follows them to a hole in the ice. All six men have entered Death's Door.

On tiny Washington Island, everyone is a neighbor, and every neighbor is a friend. The loss of even one is a loss for all.

Listen!

This is the sound of the island crying—the people and the trees and the beasts— all mourning for the friends they lost.

Whhhhhhhhhhh!

That is the howl of my wind, for I am crying, too.

Think! The islanders need safe passage from the mainland, even in winter. Even in early spring. What can they do?

A new ferry? Yes!
With a steel hull that can break through the ice
and cross Death's Door safely!
In every season!

And so it was.

A steel-hulled ferry to cross Death's Door.
A sturdy ferry, forevermore.

Long have I listened. Long have I watched.
Why do people cross my water? Because
they are human. Ambitious and restless
. . . but loving, too.

And I?

I am wind. I am water. I am rocks.
I am the keeper of stories,
the keeper of bones.

I am Death's Door.

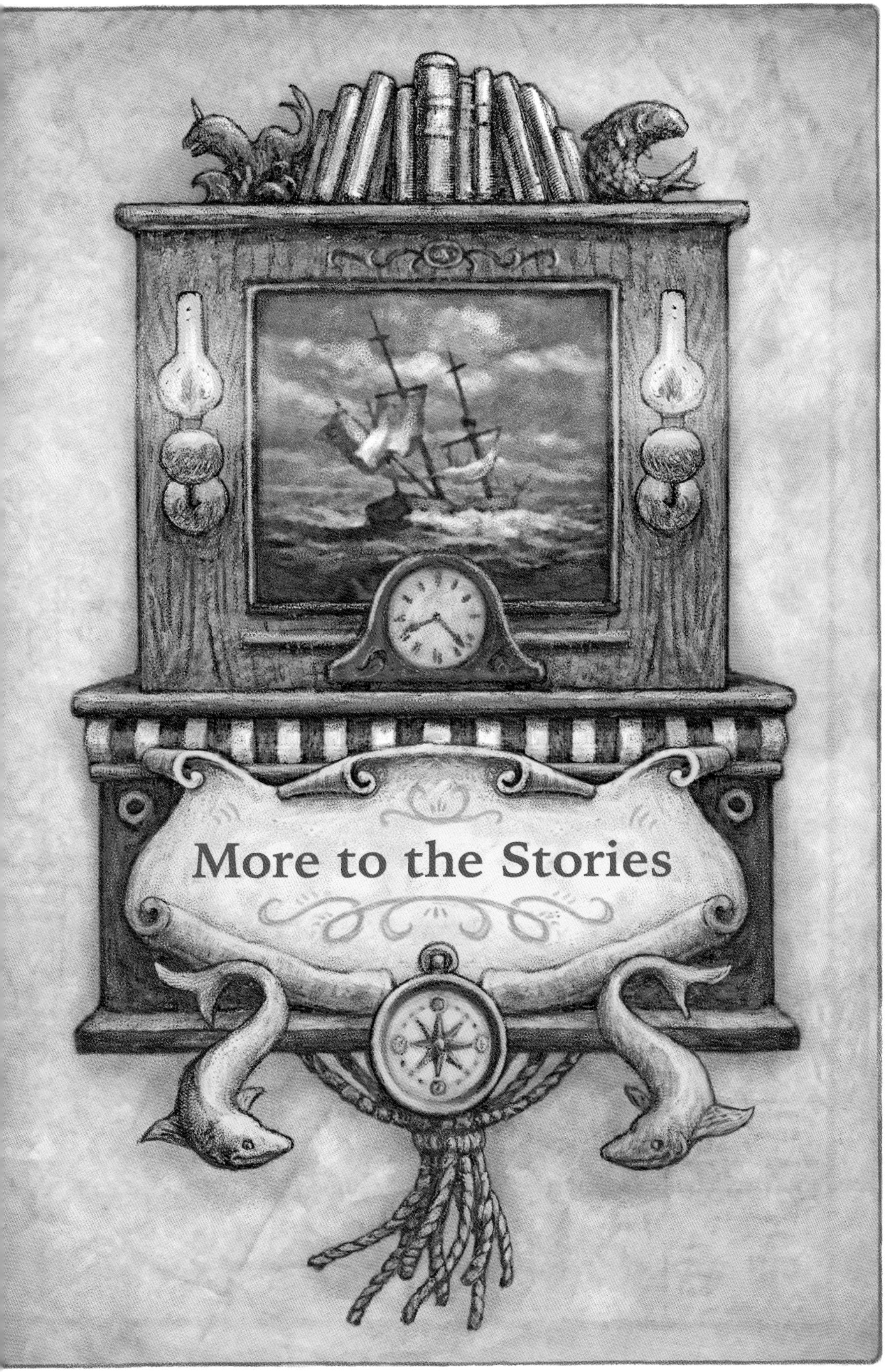
More to the Stories

Author's Note

Behind the Door: Unlocking the Secrets of "The Monster Battle"

When I uncover new historical information, it feels like I've opened a secret door. The past springs to life—and I'm smack in the middle of the action!

Most people accept one story of how Death's Door (also referred to by the French translation, *Porte des Morts*) got its name. The legend tells of a fierce battle between two American Indian tribes, resulting in the drowning of many warriors in the waters off the tip of the Door Peninsula. But there wasn't enough evidence to prove that this was the real story behind the name. Part of the challenge of unlocking history's secrets is that many events weren't recorded. In addition, early newspapers were often more interested in telling a good tale than getting the facts right. How could I find the truth?

First, I asked Samantha Smith, museum manager at the Forest County Potawatomi Cultural Center, Library, and Museum, whether she could find anything that would shed light on how the legend came to be. But Ms. Smith didn't find any records.

Then I had a conversation with a historian, Dr. Patrick Jung. He confirmed there is indeed a record of many Potawatomi who had drowned in these waters sometime between 1690 and 1763. But they were part of a trade party, not warriors. He told me about a report from a man who lived in the 1800s named Samuel Stambaugh, a government Indian agent who was familiar with the local American Indian people. Importantly, Stambaugh had nothing to gain by twisting his story. Stambaugh wrote in 1831:

The termination [end] of the Peninsula at the entrance of Green Bay into the Lake, presents [shows] a high bluff of rocks. . . . This cliff or bluff is upwards of [more than] a hundred feet high. The nearest channel to the main land . . . is known to mariners [sailors] by the name of Death's door passage. It received this name, as an Indian tradition informs us, in consequence of a circumstance occurring many years ago, by which a large body of Indians were lost near the bluff of rocks projecting [sticking out] over the lake at this point. A band of Indians in canoes, on their way to some of the French trading posts, halted at this place for the purpose of resting and taking some refreshment, and while seated on their stone table, which then projected about three feet above the surface of the water, a storm arose suddenly, which swept over the rock a tremendous sea, and dashed their canoes to pieces. The bluff of rocks was too steep to scale [climb], and the poor creatures, having no other means of escape . . . nearly all perished [died]. On the face of the rocks fifteen or twenty feet above the surface of the water, there are figures of Indians and Canoes painted in Indian fashion, which must have been done with much difficulty.

When unlocking history's secrets, we can't always find a definite answer. So we don't know positively that Dr. Jung's explanation is correct. But it is based in facts we know to be true, so it's the story I chose to tell.

Dr. Jung's knowledge of the Potawatomi trade parties allowed him to offer details for the story, including the season they would have traveled and the fact that trade parties included men, women, and children.

During our conversation, Dr. Jung mentioned that the Potawatomi people were afraid to cross an open body of water. I asked the most important question a history sleuth can ask: "Why?" Dr. Jung answered, "They were afraid of the monster, Mishepeshu, who lived beneath the water. The Potawatomi believed a storm was a great battle between Mishepeshu and the Thunderers."

Aha! The secret door of history had opened! And I was there!

Mishepeshu *and the* Thunderers

The horned figure in this rock painting is Mishepeshu. The painting is part of a sacred site in Ontario, Canada, on the shore of Lake Superior. It was painted by an Ojibwe tribal member sometime before 1850.
Agawa Rock, Panel VIII, photo by D. Gordon E. Robertson, Wikimedia Commons

The Potawatomi, Ojibwe, and Ottawa are part of a connected grou of tribes called the Anishinaabeg that shares many traditions, stories and even a language. Mishepeshu and the Thunderers are part of the Anishinaabeg tradition.

According to this tradition, Mishepeshu is a powerful spirit who lives beneath water. To satisfy him, the Anishinaabeg threw tobacco into his water. Mishepeshu' great enemies are the Thunderers, powerful storm spirits who live in the rain clouds in the western sky. Thunder is the sound of the Thunderers shouting. They can shoc bolts of lightning from their eyes.

This carving of a thunderbird (another name for Thunderer) can be found in Twin Bluffs, Wisconsin. This photograph was taken in 1936.
WHI IMAGE ID 34566